Starter

Hi!
I'm Cousin Art
And I like to start
A new thing every day.
But I never finish anything
At least that's what…
they…

Tony Bradman

D0183175

Other fantastic poetry collections from Scholastic:

FUNNY POEMS

Compiled by Jan Dean

Illustrated by Woody Fox

Visit Jan Dean's website at

www.jandean.co.uk

SCHOLASTIC

For DOMINIC DAVIES, who is keen on jokes and trumpets.

Published by Scholastic Ltd,
Book End, Range Road, Witney,
Oxfordshire OX29 0YD
www.scholastic.co.uk
Designed using Adobe InDesign

Compiled by Jan Dean
Internal illustrations by Woody Fox
Cover illustration by Tony De Saulles

Printed in Great Britain by CPI Group (UK) Ltd, Croydon, CR0 4YY
© 2015 Scholastic Ltd
1 2 3 4 5 6 7 8 9 5 6 7 8 9 0 1 2 3 4

British Library Cataloguing-in-Publication Data
A catalogue record for this book is available from the British Library.

ISBN 978-1407-15885-3

CONTENTS

NOW THERE'S A FUNNY THING...

IF I RULED THE WORLD

TOPSY-TURVINESS

TICKLE STUFF

THE LAST WORD

FIRST WORD

They wanted to hear "Mummy"
They wanted to hear "Dad"
But I fancied something altogether
Bold and big and bad.
So I goo-gooed and I ga-gahed
And gurgled like a drain
While I brewed a monster word up
In my big bad baby brain.

They waited for a word from me
And wasn't there a fuss
When the first thing that I said was
There's a duck-billed-fatty-platypus
Somersaulting underneath that bus
And I don't think I have ever seen
A creature so preposterous.
My mother promptly fainted
And my father crossed his eyes
In a quite absurd expression
of absolute surprise.

Once recovered, they ran off
To tell the world about their child
(Who was in fact a genius)
While I just sat and smiled.

When they came back with an audience
I gave them of my best –
I ga-ga-gooed and goo-ga-gahed
Then threw up on my vest.

Jan Dean

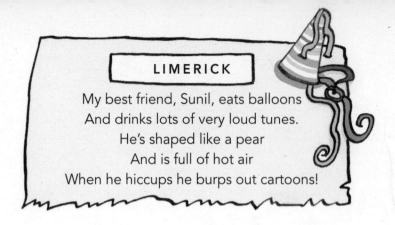

LIMERICK

My best friend, Sunil, eats balloons
And drinks lots of very loud tunes.
He's shaped like a pear
And is full of hot air
When he hiccups he burps out cartoons!

Jan Dean

PECULIAR PEOPLE

Parent's Evening

Hello, Mrs Spinner,
Now, about your son, Sam.

First of all I must say
I'm sorry to hear about your Rottweiler
Sam says it's been poorly
Well, the number of times it's eaten Sam's
  homework
I'm not surprised.
And then it gave Sam dog-flu and he was away
On the day that Brighton played Spurs in the cup
And it was a shame that he chewed Sam's PE kit
What's that?
You don't have a Rottweiler?
You don't even have a dog?
How strange.

By the way, Mrs Spinner,
May I congratulate your husband
On being chosen to represent England
In the next Olympics.
You must be very proud.

He's a shot-putter Sam says.
And Sammy tells me you're a model.
And you're in those bra commercials.
What's that?
You have to be going?
You have something to say to Sammy?
Well, lovely to meet you at last.
Tell Sammy I'm looking forward to seeing him
   tomorrow.

Goodbye, Mrs Spinner.
Goodbye.

Roger Stevens

School for Witches

2nd Witch: *Fillet of a fenny snake*
                  In the cauldron boil and bake

William Shakespeare Macbeth Act 4, Scene 1

So today, children, we will learn to make
 Fillet of a fenny snake.
Now now, Sybil, none of your moans and groans;
 Get on with it and remove those bones.

No, Mervyn, not a funny snake. Fenny!
 It comes from a fen, Kenny.
That's lovely, really disgusting, Matilda.
No dear, I don't know what killed her.

Matilda, show the others your fillet.
No, Simon. We can't grill it.
It's for our spell. Caspar, for badness' sake
Give Sybil back her fenny snake.

Give it back, child. You've got one of your own.
And leave those poisoned entrails alone.
No, Sybil. Slice lengthwise; by candlelight.
Get Nick to show you. Yes, that's right.

Lobo. Take that poisonous toad off your shoulder.
Put it in your coursework folder.
I've told you ninety-nine times. You know the rule:
No pets. No pets allowed in school.

Careful, Nostrodomus, don't spill that slime!
Where's my hourglass? Is that the time!?
Everything away! Whooshsky-cadabra! That's right!
Or we won't be home before midnight.

You've all been ever so bad today.
So tomorrow I'll give you an hour's play
While I bake the snake. But look at that sky!
Badnight, witchlets. I must fly.

Gerard Benson

That Sort of Mood

I'm a fish.
I glanced in the bathroom mirror
And there I was – a haddock,
My mouth turned down
And my gills all droopy.
So I practised a few fish faces in the glass,
Blew a few bubbles
Then swam downstairs to make a cup of tea.

Jan Dean

Mazey Mary

Lazy Mary Scatterbocker
eating chilly chockablocker
licks a glory jellyrocker
sips a super shlushimocker
from a mucky bucket.

Joan Poulson

A Mother's Confession

(Or: What you have always suspected...)

As soon as you are asleep in bed
I unlock the secret cupboard
Where I keep all the chocolate
And I eat it and eat it and eat it.
I don't share it with anybody
And I don't give half a hoot about my teeth.

As soon as you are tucked all tidy in your bed
I put my feet up on the sofa – shoes still on,
Or if I take them off I don't undo the laces first,
Then I drink fizzy cans and eat crisps,
And practise blowing huge, round, pink bubbles
Out of hubba-bubba gum.

Once you're asleep
I watch *those* programmes on the telly
(The ones I always say are trash)
And I don't go to bed at a sensible time –
Even though I'm really, really tired.
I don't go because I'm a grown-up
And I can do what I like
And you can't stop me.
Ha. Ha. Ha.

Jan Dean

Uncle Frank

When we're all asleep in bed,
My Uncle Frank unscrews his head.
He fixes on another one
And sets off for a night of fun.

It really gave me quite a jolt,
The first time that I saw the bolt,
Which Uncle proudly showed to me
In the cellar after tea.

He says the reason for his fame
Is that we share a famous name:
Oh, I forgot to tell you mine,
Our family name is Frankenstein.

John Foster

DAY
HEAD

Cool at the Pool

Roll my muscles
Round the swimming pool
Make the girls goggle
Feel real cool.

Flex my pecs
Swagger and pose
Look real tough
Look down my nose.

Walk to the deep end
They all stare
My red shiny trunks
My real trendy hair.

Stand on the diving board
Think I'll jump in
Just one problem
I can't swim.

David Harmer

Who's Who?

Jemima Pugh never knew
a crocodile from an alligator.
So poor Miss Pugh didn't have a clue
which wriggled up the bank and ate her.

Alison Chisholm

Auntie Arabella

Auntie Arabella grows
Geraniums between her toes.

Twining round her legs and knees
Are various colours of sweet peas.

Sitting stately on her tum
Is a gold chrysanthemum.

Sprouting from her bulbous nose
Is a beautiful red rose.

Lovingly, my Uncle Ted
Tends her in her flower bed.

John Foster

Old Hank

For a lark,
For a prank,
Old Hank
Walked a plank.
These bubbles mark
 O
 O
 O
 O
 O
Where Hank sank.

Anon

What a Sucker!

As a glassblower, Septimus Grayling
Had a rather regrettable failing.
When they laid him to rest,
He'd a PANE in his chest –
'stead of blowing, he kept on inhaling.

Graham Denton

Colonel Fazackerley

Colonel Fazackerley Butterworth-Toast
Bought an old castle complete with a ghost,
But someone or other forgot to declare
To Colonel Fazack that the spectre was there.

On the very first evening, while waiting to dine,
The colonel was taking a fine sherry wine,
When the ghost, with a furious flash and a flare,
Shot out of the chimney and shivered, "Beware!"

Colonel Fazackerley put down his glass
And said, "My dear fellow, that's really first class!
I just can't conceive how you do it at all.
I imagine you're going to a Fancy Dress Ball?"

At this, the dread host gave a withering cry.
Said the Colonel (his monocle firm in his eye),
"Now just how you do it I wish I could think.
Do sit down and tell me, and please have a drink."

The ghost in his phosphorous cloak gave a roar
And floated about between ceiling and floor.
He walked through a wall and returned through
    a pane
And backed up the chimney and came
    down again.

Said the Colonel, "With laughter I'm feeling
    quite weak!"
(As trickles of merriment ran down his cheek).
"My house-warming party I hope you won't spurn.
You must say you'll come and you'll give us
    a turn!"

At this, the poor spectre – quite out of his wits –
Proceeded to shake himself almost to bits.
He rattled his chains and he clattered his bones
And he filled the whole castle with mumbles
    and moans.

But Colonel Fazackerley, just as before,
Was simply delighted and called out "Encore!"
At which the ghost vanished, his efforts in vain,
And never was seen at the castle again.

"Oh dear, what a pity!" said Colonel Fazack.
"I don't know his name, so I can't call him back."
And then with a smile that was hard to define,
Colonel Fazackerley went in to dine.

Charles Causley

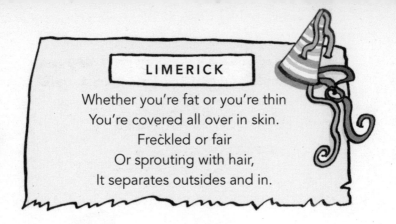

LIMERICK

Whether you're fat or you're thin
You're covered all over in skin.
Freckled or fair
Or sprouting with hair,
It separates outsides and in.

Jan Dean

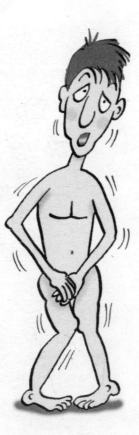

NOW THERE'S A FUNNY THING...

Trying to Hide the Really Rude SNOG Words

Some very rude words are hiding
in this poem, it**'s not**
too hard to **spotty face** most of them
this line's about Steve Stanton's dam**p ants**
and how slic**k Nick**, **er**, snores sometimes.

This verse is all about
being behind dum**b um**brellas
how we **toil et**c in the classroom
go home and ea**t rump** steak and **peas**.

Some of the really rude words
won't **SNOG** stay out of sight at all
they keep on **POOH** jumping
from behind their **WIDDLE** disguises
which seems to me
very bad **BURP** manners indeed.

They should keep quiet
big fat face up to things, it's not
difficult to hide a **wee** word or two
if you **BOTTY BURPS** try
where there's a **will**, **ee** – there's a way.

David Harmer

Property for Sale

Two houses up for sale.
One stick, one straw.
Both self-assembly.
See pig next door.

Rachel Rooney

Three Silly Things to Do with a Sock

1. Fill it with custard –
   Lovely yellow stuff.
   It will seep through the knitting
   And gum up the fluff.

2. Wear it on your ear.
   Let it wave and flap.
   Or balance it on the top of your head,
   And say it is a cap.

3. Cook it for your tea,
   Eat it with ketchup and with chips.
   To show that you've enjoyed it
   Be sure to lick your lips.

Jan Dean

Bebe Belinda & Carl Columbus

There was a girl who threw bananas about
When she couldn't get bananas she threw baseball
  bats about
When she couldn't get baseball bats she threw big
  blue beehives about
And her name was Bebe, Bebe Belinda.

There was a boy who threw cuckoo clocks about
When he couldn't find cuckoo clocks he threw
  cucumbers about
When he couldn't find cucumbers he went crackers
  and threw christening cakes about
And his name was Carl, Carl Columbus.

In Hanover Terrace, that magical place
Bebe and Carl met face to red face.
She bust his cuckoo clock with a bunch of bananas
In a swashbuckling sword fight his cucumber cutlass
Carved her baseball bat to bits.
She bashed him on the bonce with her best blue
  beehive
But he craftily crowned her with a christening cake.

And they left it to me, old Lizzie Lush
To clean up the street with my scrubbing brush.

Adrian Mitchell

George Who Played with a Dangerous Toy and Suffered a Catastrophe of Considerable Dimensions

When George's Grandmama was told
That George had been a good as Gold,
She Promised in the Afternoon
To buy him an *Immense* BALLOON.
And so she did; but when it came,
It got into the candle flame,
And being of a dangerous sort
Exploded with a Loud Report!
The Lights went out! The Windows broke!
The Room was filled with reeking smoke!
And in the darkness shrieks and yells
Were mingled with Electric Bells,
And falling masonry and groans
And crunching as of broken bones,
And dreadful shrieks, when, worst of all,
The House itself began to fall!
It tottered, shuddering to and fro,
Then crashed into the street below –
Which happened to be Savile Row.

When help arrived, among the Dead
Were Cousin Mary, Little Fred,
The Footmen (both of them), the Groom,
The man who cleaned the Billiard Room,
The Chaplain, and the Still-Room Maid.
And I am dreadfully afraid
That Monsieur Champignon, the Chef,
Will now be permanently deaf –
And both his Aides are much the same;
While George, who was in part to blame,
Received, you will regret to hear,
A nasty lump behind the ear.

The moral is that little Boys
Should not be given dangerous Toys.

Hilaire Belloc

There Was a Young Man of Bengal

There was a young man of Bengal
Who went to a fancy-dress ball,
He went, just for fun
Dressed up as a bun
And a dog ate him up in the hall.

Anon

After the Football Match

Harry had to carry:
a football,
his trainers,
his shin guards,
and hold up his shorts
– the elastic had just snapped
at the end of the game!
Suddenly it started to rain
so Harry started to run
then it began to pour
so Harry began to run faster
but
he started to drop things:
a football,
his trainers,
his shin guards,
and finally
– just as he passed the girls' netball
match – his **shorts**!

Ian Souter

Hey Diddle Diddle

Hey diddle diddle, the cat and the fiddle,
The cow jumped over the moon.
The little dog laughed to see such fun
And the dish ran away with the chocolate
  biscuits.

Michael Rosen

April Fool in School

Miss Hall come quick
I swear it's true
A MONKEY
In the infants' loo.
And over in the library
A CROCODILE
Is drinking tea.
SOME SEALS
Are swimming in the hall
They're playing with a basketball,
And in the corridor I swear
The most enormous
GRIZZLY BEAR.

Is all this happening in our school?
Of course it's not, you
APRIL FOOL!

Ian Bland

An Accident Happened to My Brother Jim

An accident happened to my brother Jim,
When somebody threw a tomato at him.
Tomatoes are juicy and soft to the skin,
But this one was specially wrapped. In a tin.

Anon

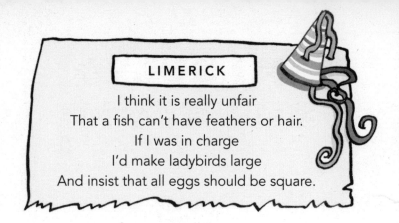

LIMERICK

I think it is really unfair
That a fish can't have feathers or hair.
If I was in charge
I'd make ladybirds large
And insist that all eggs should be square.

Jan Dean

IF I RULED THE WORLD

Advice for Staging Your Own Olympic Games

Never play volleyball with a bag of flour
Never use Mum's hairbrush as a baton in the
  relay race
The flower bed is not a sandpit for the long jump
And remember – the Olympic Games does not
  include kiss-chase

Never pole-vault in the vicinity of
  Grandpa's greenhouse
Never throw the discus using Mum's best plates
The broom handle is not a pole – nor is it a javelin
Never use flowerpots (especially if they have
  flowers in) for weights

Your dog is a dog, not a horse
Although, at a push, could be used for
  equestrian events
Do not use the duvet covers in the
  airing cupboard
To make those big marquee-type tents

Never use The Complete Set of Jamie Oliver for
  the winners' podium
Never bribe the judges with crisps, chocolate,
  football cards or cash.
And finally when Mum comes home to find her
  house and garden in a mess
Say, Excuse me, but I'm in the hundred metres –
  must dash!

Roger Stevens

If Things Grew Down

If things grew down
instead of up,
A dog would grow
Into a pup.
A cat would grow
Into a kitten.
Your sweater would grow
Into a mitten.
A cow would grow
Into a calf
And a whole would grow
Into a half.
Big would grow
Into something small
And small would grow
Into nothing at all.

Robert D Hoeft

A Charm to Make Your PE Teacher's Football Boots 3 Sizes Smaller

(While he is wearing them...)

Stand on one leg and say "Oooo!"
Stand on the other. Say "Aaaah..."
Then shout – "Feet, you stink – poo!
           Boots, I shrink you!"
Then the walls of his boots
Will come leathering in
Like a boa constrictor
Squeezing his skin.
Imagine your teacher's wriggly toes
All squashed together in two pink rows.
The harder you wish it
The tighter you'll squish it.
This spell is probably your only chance
Of making your teacher ballet dance!

Jan Dean

What the Headteacher Said When He Saw Me Running Out of School at 1.15 p.m. on 21 July Last Year to Buy an Ice Cream from Pelozzi's Van

Hey!*

Fred Sedgwick

* This poem is an attempt on three world records at once: the longest title, the longest footnote and the shortest text of any poem in the Western world. It has been lodged with the Guinness Book of Records.

No Chance

When I put my tooth under my pillow
The Tooth Fairy leaves me some money.
If I borrow a spare set of Grandma's teeth
Will the Tooth Fairy think that it's funny?

Muriel Berry

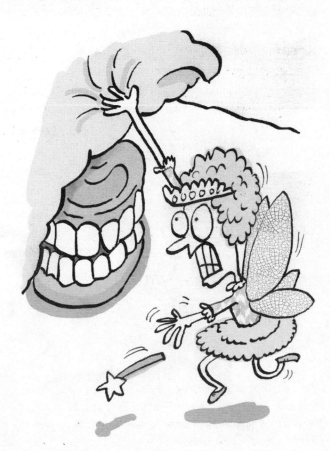

Don't Call Alligator Long-Mouth Till You Cross the River

Call alligator long-mouth
call alligator saw-mouth
call alligator pushy-mouth
call alligator scissors-mouth
call alligator raggedy-mouth
call alligator bumpy-bum
call alligator all dem rude word
but better wait

till you cross river.

John Agard

A Tip for Feeding Piranhas

Piranhas ignore chips
Scraped off of your plate

And pudding with custard
Apparently hate.

Though sent strangely frenzied
By tomato ketchup

Baked beans they've swallowed
They very soon retch up.

So what holds appeal
For my fishy friends then?

I've now only nine
Where I used to have ten!

Philip Waddell

You Must Never Bath in an Irish Stew

You must never bath in an Irish stew
It's a most illogical thing to do.
   But should you persist against my reasoning
   Don't fail to add the appropriate seasoning.

Spike Milligan

Oh, You Shouldn't Have!

I bought you a cauliflower.
I thought a rose
Was too much the same sort of red as your nose.

I brought you a radish.
I thought a cake
Was a little too much for your waistline to take.

I brought you a haddock
I thought you'd prefer
A fish to a flower – to show that I care.

I would have brought perfumed silk sheets for
    your bed
But I didn't, so here is a bullfrog instead.

Jan Dean

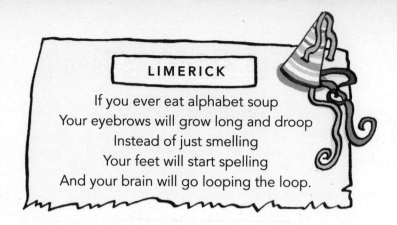

LIMERICK

If you ever eat alphabet soup
Your eyebrows will grow long and droop
Instead of just smelling
Your feet will start spelling
And your brain will go looping the loop.

Jan Dean

WEIRD WORDS

Hug a Slug!

I could
tug a rug,
glug a plug,
slug a thug,
lug a jug
and even
mug a bug
but hug a slug?
YYUUUGGG!

Ian Souter

Spelling Test

I've stood in this queue
To go to the lueue
Since quarter past tueue.
It's perfectly trueue
– Oh what shall I dueue?

Andy Seed

Tut-Tut

Walked into the clothes shop,
what did I see?
There on a large sign,
right in front of me:

MENSWEAR

Further round the clothes shop
what did I see?
On a second large sign,
right in front of me:

WOMENSWEAR

Walking out that clothes shop
what did I see?
Yet another large sign,
right in front of me:

CHILDRENSWEAR

Well they shouldn't.

David Horner

I Can't Think Straight!

I can't think straight!
    That's good.
    You see,
    You're having
  An attack
  Of poetry.
So think curly,
Think cock-eyed,
Think round corners,
Round the outside.
Think criss-cross
Or in figures-of-eight
But whatever you do –
Don't think straight!

Sue Cowling

Animal Instincts

Wow, you really **wolf** your food down, don't you?
  Do I?
Did you know you snuffle like a **boar**?
  I do?
Hey, you're looking a bit pale around the **gills**.
  Really?
Gosh, you look **dog** tired.
  What?
Perhaps you should take a **cat** nap.
  Eh?
And why are you getting all **crabby**?
  Now look here, you **beastly thing**
  don't you make a **monkey** out of me!
  I was having a **whale** of a time
  before you got all **pig-headed**
  stuck your **beak** in
  and started **rabbit**ing on.
  Now please **buzz** off!

James Carter

I Sometimes Think

I sometimes think I'd rather crow
And be a rooster than to roost
And be a crow. But I dunno.

A rooster he can roost also,
Which don't seem fair when crows
can't crow.
Which may help some. Still I dunno.

Crows should be glad of one thing, though;
Nobody thinks of eating crow,
While roosters they are good enough
For anyone unless they're tough.

There are lots of tough old roosters though,
And anyway a crow can't crow,
So mebby roosters stand more show.
It looks that way. But I dunno.

Anon

An Odd Kettle of Fish

1. The detective said that
   the books had been cooked.
   (They tasted good.)

2. My teacher said we could
   have a free hand.
   (I added it to my collection.)

3. Some people bottle up
   their feelings.
   (I keep mine in a jar.)

4. My mother said
   "Hold your tongue!"
   (It was too slippery.)

5. When my sister laughs
   she drives me round the bend.
   (I catch the bus back.)

6. Dad told me
   to keep a stiff upper lip.
   (It's in a box by my bed.)

7. My Uncle is a terrible
    name dropper.
    (I help my Aunt to sweep them up.)

8. In the school races
    I licked everyone in class
    (It made my tongue sore.)

Pie Corbett

Unbelievable Sports Facts!

Tennis one more than nine.

Badminton is an evil form of goodminton.

If you go round a track twice on a bike you're recycling.

Grasshoppers like cricket.

When wildebeest paddle small boats they're gnuing.

Hearse racing is dead good.

Last year they compared all the motorsports and Formula won.

Crossing the Atlantic on a 747 is not plane sailing.

A donkey once appeared at the Badminton Horse Trials – it was found guilty.

Unbelievable!

Andy Seed

Three Frazzles in a Frimple

1 snunk in a snuncle
2 gripes in a grimp
3 frazzles in a frimple
4 blips in a blimp
5 nips in a nimple
6 nerps in a neep
7 gloops in a gloople
8 flurps in a fleap
9 snozzles in a snoozle
10 leaps in a bunny
some sums are ridiculous
and some sums are funny.

Brian Patten

Combinations

A flea flew by a bee. The bee
To flee the flea, flew by a fly.
The fly flew high to flee the bee
Who flew to flee the flea who flew
To flee the fly who now flew by.

The bee flew by the fly. The fly
To flee the bee, flew by the flea.
The flea flew high to flee the fly
Who flew to flee the bee who flew
To flee the flea who now flew by.

The fly flew by the flea. The flea
To flee the fly, flew by the bee.
The bee flew high to flee the flea
Who flew to flee the fly who flew
To flee the bee who now flew by.

The flea flew by the fly. The fly
To flee the flea, flew by the bee.
The bee flew high to flee the fly
Who flew to flee the flea who flew
To flee the bee who now flew by.

The fly flew by the bee. The bee
To flee the fly, flew by the flea.
The flea flew high to flee the bee
Who flew to flee the fly who flew
To flee the flea who now flew by.

The bee flew by the flea. The flea
To flee the bee, flew by the fly.
The fly flew high to flee the flea
Who flew to flee the bee who flew
To flee the fly who now flew by.

Mary Ann Hoberman

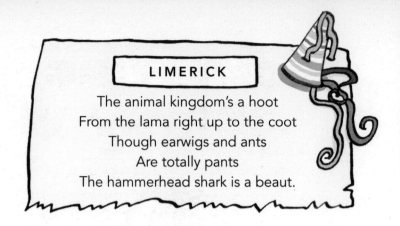

LIMERICK

The animal kingdom's a hoot
From the lama right up to the coot
Though earwigs and ants
Are totally pants
The hammerhead shark is a beaut.

Jan Dean

MONKEYING AROUND

The Wildebeest

Though wonderful, the wildebeest's
not quite the brightest of the beasts.

One problem is – you'll never guess –
it can't recall its own address.

It wanders west, it wanders east –
it makes no difference in the least.

The wildebeest's now so depressed
the doctor's prescribed pills for stress.

But, though with frowns its brow is creased,
its wanderings have never ceased.

And all around the wilderness
it walks in its bewilderedness.

David Horner

Muddled Minibeasts

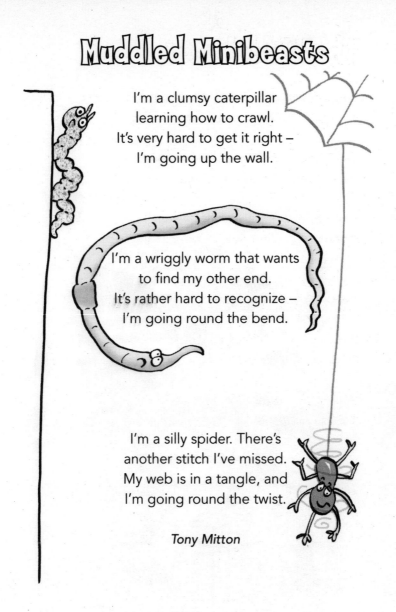

I'm a clumsy caterpillar
learning how to crawl.
It's very hard to get it right –
I'm going up the wall.

I'm a wriggly worm that wants
to find my other end.
It's rather hard to recognize –
I'm going round the bend.

I'm a silly spider. There's
another stitch I've missed.
My web is in a tangle, and
I'm going round the twist.

Tony Mitton

At the Match

They didn't like my earwig,
the reason I don't know…
But at the match they chanted
earwig go, earwig go, earwig go…

Liz Brownlee

Overheard on Safari

Look!
There's a flock of elephants
Galumphing across the horizon.

Herd of elephants.

Of course I've heard of elephants.
I was just telling you.
I saw a flock of them over there.

Herd!

Not from here you can't have.
Unless you've got sharper ears than
  mine.
You can't hear them from here,
Even a big flock like that.

It's a HERD of elephants!

Yes I know. Of course it is,
I've got eyes in my head.
I was just pointing them out to you.

Gerard Benson

In a Cage in a Zanzibar Zoo

In a cage in a Zanzibar zoo
You will find a polite cockatoo,
    Who never says "Hoy!"
    or "Watcher, my boy,"
But "How-do-you-do-do-you-do?"

Gerard Benson

The Newt

Brown as a root
In his dark spotted suit,
The Common Newt's
Uncommonly cute.

Gill McEvoy

Lice Are Nice

Head lice are not loners
We're quite a friendly bunch,
That's why we swap our owners
When they all sit down for lunch.

Rachel Rooney

The Termite

Some primal termite knocked on wood
And tasted it and found it good
And that is why your Cousin May
Fell through the parlour floor today.

Ogden Nash

Downside

Having a puppy is super dooper
(apart from the bit with the pooper scooper...)

Jan Dean

Lovesick Snail

A giant African land snail
has fallen in love with our teacher,
his eyes are out on stalks, you can tell
he's besotted, this lovelorn creature.
If you look closely you'll see him
blowing kisses across the room,
this giant African land snail with a crush
and no hope of lifting his gloom.
And we really couldn't blame him,
our teacher is awfully nice.
We know for a fact that she's also adored
by stick insects, gerbils and mice.

Brian Moses

Rhyme-osaur the Dinosaur

Out of a deep dark mine-osaur
at roughly half past nine-osaur
there came a sleepy steg-osaur
into the warm sunshine-osaur
he warmed his chilly spine-osaur
which made him feel divine-osaur
he nibbled on a pine-osaur
and drank a glass of wine-osaur
but then he saw a sign-osaur
which made him yelp and whine-osaur
it forecast his decline-osaur
his time had come to die-nosaur

John Rice

All Goats Munch

All goats munch
But these goats munch the most,
As leading lunch-time munchers
They can quickly make a ghost
Of thistles, pies or toast!
They'll munch on breakfast fry-ups,
They'll munch on Sunday roasts,
They'll even munch on ladies' hats
Or fancy petticoats!

And though –
They do not wish to boast,
As super munch crunchers,
As leading lunch-time munchers
These goats munch the most!

John Cotton

Baboons' Bottoms

Baboons' bottoms
Are so rude,
Red and shiny
And so nude:
Lumpy bumpy,
With a laugh
They flash them
For each photograph!

Baboons' bottoms
Bright and lewd,
Blue and yucky,
Oh so crude!
I think my aunty
Would be more happy
If they were made to wear a nappy!

Baboons' bottoms,
What a sight!
Designed to give
Your gran a fright;
Who can't believe the age-old rumour
That God has got
A sense of humour!

Coral Rumble

A Baby Sardine

A baby Sardine
Saw her first submarine:
She was scared and watched through a
  peephole.

"Oh, come, come, come,"
Said the Sardine's mum,
"It's only a tin full of people."

Spike Milligan

Suddenly – at the Dining Table

"Dear Mum…" gasped the viper,
"I will not pull through…
So I want to say Mum…
How much I love you.
And Dad," groaned the serpent…
"It's time I confessed
What long I have meant to…
Dear Dad…you're the best!
And sweet little brother
As now I depart
This mortal coil…
Promise a place in your heart.
And now…" wheezed the viper
With weakening lung,
"Call the undertaker…
I've bitten my tongue."

Philip Waddell

Frog Dreams

I want to be a bumble frog
Not any old green humble frog
On any old wet rotting log
I want to be a fuzzy frog
Not any old green scuzzy frog
On any old wet mouldering log
Why should bees have all the fun –
With stripes and wings that catch the sun?
Frogs are just green, fat and funny
But I've ambitions to make honey…

Jan Dean

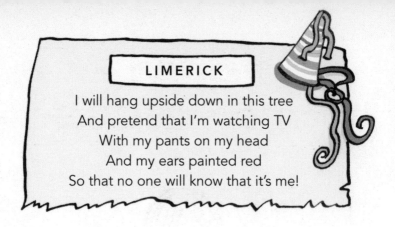

LIMERICK

I will hang upside down in this tree
And pretend that I'm watching TV
With my pants on my head
And my ears painted red
So that no one will know that it's me!

Jan Dean

TOPSY-
TURVINESS

World of Weird

In the World of Weird
all the girls wear beards
and the boys keep bees in their beds
the girls dig holes and live like moles
and the boys grow trees on their heads

In the World of Weird
all the oranges are blue
and the lemons are as sweet as can be
bananas are round, and grow in the
   ground
or down at the bottom of the sea

In the World of Weird
all the fish can fly
and the chips are fried in lakes
the dogs love cats: with sauce, of course
served up on silver plates

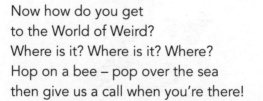

Now how do you get
to the World of Weird?
Where is it? Where is it? Where?
Hop on a bee – pop over the sea
then give us a call when you're there!

James Carter

The Weatherman Forgets His Glasses

Yellow.

Hooray will be rowdy
with a dance of hours.
Some of these flowers
could be hobnail.
The ten preachers
will be formal for the tying up here.

There will be slier tame teachers
in the yeast with only
mental cheeses.
In the vest
there will be swarms
of wonder and frightening.

True sorrow
the leather will start silly
with a whisk of pain.
This train will be fried bread
waiter. Murder forth
this drain will be off show
with wizards in the fountains.
The tinned peaches
will be very slow.

The day will be funnier
in the mouth
with just a glance of frog
in the great laughter moon.

That's all together.

So cry miaow.

David Horner

Gorbelly Button and His Daddy Gorbelly

Gorbelly Button and his daddy
Gorbelly
live in a house called
Shimble Shambelly
which is just down the road, not far from
Dalmelly
where the kids are sweet but the babies
are
smelly

It's a very large house is
Shimble Shambelly
with its huge living room and its wide
screen
telly
and their housekeeper's name is Katie
Ann
Kelly
but she smells rather strange, like a
soaking wet
welly

Now eat up your food says daddy
Gorbelly
you must drink the sea and eat beaches
that are
shelly
eat up your sharks, your fishes made of
jelly
for you'll want to be like me and have a
ginormous
belly

John Rice

Snowman School Rules

1. NEVER talk to children. They may try to take you indoors.
2. DO NOT fall about laughing at the accessories you are given to wear.
3. Buttons (if provided) are to be kept polished.
4. Be proud of having a carrot for a nose!
5. Resist the urge to swat at robins for being cheeky.
6. Remain awake the day after a Snow Ball to avoid rousing suspicion.
7. When the thaw comes, melt gracefully.

Sue Cowling

Moon Theory

Some scientists set out to prove
the moon is made of cheese;
the evidence they discover means
that everyone agrees

The surface of the moon
has bubbled into craters
caused, they think, by heating cheese
that's been through giant graters.

Satisfied that they are right,
the scientists now boast
that, some day soon, they're sure to find
a planet made of toast.

Celia Warren

In the Jelly Jungle

In the jelly jungle
Wild beasts and snakes
Make their dens in ice-cream caves
And sleep on chocolate cakes.

In the jelly jungle
The sausage-roll bird sings
Lays its eggs in spaghetti nests
And preens its syrup wings.

In the jelly jungle
The crocodile will doze
In a swamp of custard
With a cherry on his nose.

Jan Dean

In Trouble Again

Will you PLEASE
stop sniffing and blow your nose
tidy your things away
and hang up your clothes!
Please do something useful
like cleaning the hamster's cage
but most of all, Dad,
PLEASE just act your age!

Susan Quinn

Mum for a Day

Mum's ill in bed today
so I said I'd do the housework
and look after things.
She told me it was really hard
but I said it would be dead easy.

So...
I hoovered up the sink
Dusted the cat
Cooked my dad's shoes
Washed the carpet in the dishwasher
Fed all the ornaments and pictures
Polished the steak and kidney pudding and chips
Ironed all the letters and parcels
Posted all the shirts and knickers
And last of all...
I hung the budgie out on the washing line to dry.

It took me all day
but I got everything finished
and I was really tired.

I'm glad Mum isn't ill every day
And do you know what?

So is the budgie.

Paul Cookson

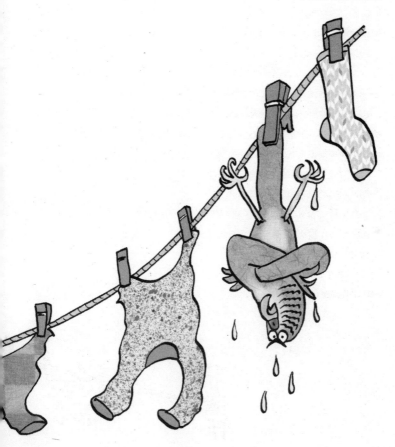

When I Was a Pirate

And when I was a pirate
One of my legs was wooden
Since then it's grown back again
Though doctors said it couldn't.

And when I was a pirate
I'd a parrot that could talk.
But now I'm Dad to seven kids
who only screech and squawk.

And when I was a pirate
I sailed the seven seas,
But now I wait at bus stops
And shop at Sainsbury's.

And when I was a pirate
I owned a treasure chest,
But now I get a weekly wage
And bank it with NatWest.

And when I was a pirate
I'd a coat with buttons of gold
But now I wear an anorak
With the hood up when it's cold.

And when I was a pirate
I'd a hook fixed on my wrist
But swapped it with a fisherman
For the fingers in his fist.

And when I was a pirate
I was hairy with a beard,
But now my head is shiny
And my hair has disappeared.

And when I was a pirate
I was merciless and cruel…
And I still am, because I make
My children go to school!

Nick Toczek

If All the World Were Paper

If all the world were paper
And all the sea were ink
If all the trees were bread and cheese
What should we have to drink?

Anon

Cupboard Love

Dumpling, how much do you love me?
A kilo of sugar, a packet of tea.

You are the apple of my eye,
my tutti frutti, my cherry pie.

You're my sticky currant bun,
my honey-pot, my candy-plum.

You've guessed by now, my very sweet,
I love you quite enough to eat.

Bettina Jones

The Twins

In form and feature, face and limb
I grew so like my brother,
That folks got taking me for him
And each for one another.
It puzzled all my kith and kin,
It reached an awful pitch;
For one of us was born a twin,
Yet not a soul knew which.

One day (to make the matter worse),
Before our names were fixed,
As we were being washed by nurse
We got completely mixed;
And thus, you see, by Fate's decree,
(Or rather nurse's whim)
My brother John got christened me
And I got christened him.

This fatal likeness even dogged
My footsteps when at school,
And I was always getting flogged,
For John turned out a fool.
I put this question hopelessly
To everyone knew –
What would you do if you were me,
To prove that you were you?
Our close resemblance turned the tide
Of my domestic life;

For somehow my intended bride
Became my brother's wife.
In short, year after year the same
Absurd mistakes went on;
And when I died – the neighbours came
And buried brother John!

Henry S Leigh

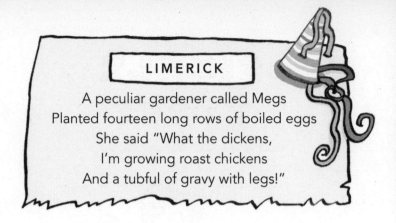

LIMERICK

A peculiar gardener called Megs
Planted fourteen long rows of boiled eggs
She said "What the dickens,
I'm growing roast chickens
And a tubful of gravy with legs!"

Jan Dean

TICKLE
STUFF

Tomato Ketchup

If you do not shake the bottle.
None'll come and then a lot'll...

Anon

Silly Question

"Why is your pram full of holly?
There should be a baby inside."

"My baby is noisy and smelly
And the holly's enjoying the ride."

Sue Cowling

Against Broccoli

The local groceries are all out of broccoli;
Loccoli.

Roy Blount Jnr

The Doctor Fell in a Deep Well

The doctor fell in a deep well
And broke his collar bone.
The Moral: Doctor, mind the sick
And leave the well alone.

Anon

The Holding Your Breath Contest

We held a Hold Your Breath contest
Me, Sammy, Shaun and Sid
Sid held his breath for a fortnight.

We're going to miss that kid.

Roger Stevens

What's Your Name?

What's your name?
I'm Daniel Frickle.
All my vests and trousers
tickle.
At the start
of every term
how I fidget!
How I squirm!

"Daniel, won't you
please sit still?"

But I itch
and itch until
school is over...
Then I run
home, with EVERYTHING

U
  N
    D
      O
        N
          E...

Jean Kenward

The Great Eating-Jelly-Through-a-Straw Contest

Under starters orders now –
    Stand by your jellies!
    Straws up!
They're off!

And Hosepipe Annie's in the lead...
But only half a lick behind is Jack the Gulp.
He's overtaking!
And on the outside Gargling Lil is guzzling
Faster than a blowtorch melting snow.
Wow. It's neck and neck –
Just watch that jell-o go!

They're in their stride now.
Slurping solid. Suck and pucker all the way –
Vacuuming that slippy slop
Right up.

Stop! Stop! The referee has pulled the plug.
Gargling Lil is gulping down her final glug.
Jack's had it. Out of it. The paramedics think it's
    jelly-shock.
And Annie wins the day!!!!

The crowd goes wild:
Their cry goes up –
Oh, Annie! You are the nation's favourite child.
Let fanfares blare! Let fireworks flare!
Let golden flags and banners be unfurled
For Hosepipe Annie –
Jelly-Eating Champion of the World!

Jan Dean

Circus Accidents

1. The Trapeze Artist
I can juggle with eggs
while I hang by my legs
from the height of the flying trapeze.
I can tickle my nose
with the tips of my toes –
DISASTER! I'm going to sneeze…

2. The High Diver
Ladies and gentlemen,
hold your breath:
Daring Dan
will dice with death.

He'll dive from a height
of a hundred feet
to land in a bucket
nice and neat.

But halfway down
Dan's in a spin:
he's forgotten to put
the water in!

Tony Mitton

Hindsight

Yesterday
I went to get my hindsight tested.
It was perfect.
Looking back,
I should have known that.

Andy Seed

Frog Street

(Frog Street is a small village in Essex)

Do they look at the world
through big bulgy eyes
in Frog Street?

Do they eat their burgers
with flies not fries
in Frog Street?

Do they sleep like a log
or under a log?
Are they looking out
for princesses to snog?

Do they have slimy bodies
and small webbed feet?
Tell me, who on earth lives
in Frog Street?

Brian Moses

Holiday Print

There was a young man from Dundee
Who had a great passion to ski,
He skied with aggression,
And left an impression –
The shape of himself on a tree!

Coral Rumble

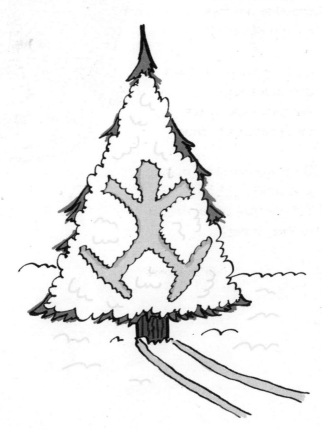

Sun a-shine, Rain a-fall

Sun a-shine, an rain-fall,
The Devil an him wife cyan 'gree at all,
The two o' them want one fish head,
The Devil call him wife bonehead.
She hiss her teeth, call him cock-eye,
Greedy, worthless an' workshy,
While them busy callin' name.
The puss walk in, say is a shame
To see a nice fish go to was'e
Lef' with a big grin on him face.

Valerie Bloom

THE LAST WORD

is beer.
Well, *zythum*, which is Ancient Egyptian beer.

Almost the last word
is *zugzwang*,
which is a seriously clever *gotcha* move in chess.
Though I suppose you could zugzwang anyone
or anything if you were smart enough.
– Sorry, Mum I can't tidy my room just now
because 1 have to do my homework
which is watching the adverts on TV –
Now that's a zugzwang.

Then there's *zucchini*
A kind of courgette.
Mum stands over me till I eat mine.
When it's zucchini I'm totally
zugzwanged.
I'd rather be a zonked zombie than
a zugwanged zucchini eater
But then, you can't win 'em all.

Jan Dean

Acknowledgements

The publishers gratefully acknowledge permission to reproduce the following copyright material:

Catherine Benson for the use of 'School for Witches' and 'Overheard on Safari' from *Omba Bolomba* by Gerard Benson. © 2005, Gerard Benson (2005, Smith/Doorstop Books).

Catherine Benson for the use of 'In a Cage in a Zanzibar Zoo' by Gerard Benson.

Muriel Berry for the use of 'No Chance'.

Ian Bland for the use of 'April Fool in School'.

Liz Brownlee for the use of 'At the Match' by Liz Brownlee from *Shouting at the Ocean* by Graham Denton. © 2009, Liz Brownlee (2009, Hands Up Books).

Caroline Sheldon Literary Agency for the use of 'Don't Call Alligator Long-mouth Till You Cross the River' from *Say It Again, Granny* by John Agard. © 1986, John Agard (1986, Random House).

James Carter for the use of 'Animal Instincts' and 'World of Weird'.

Alison Chisholm for the use of 'Who's Who?'.

Paul Cookson for the use of 'Mum for a Day'.

Pie Corbett for the use of 'A Odd Kettle of Fish'.

Sue Cowling for the use of 'Snowman School Rules', 'I Can't Think Straight!' and 'Silly Question'.

David Higham Associates for the use of 'Circus Accidents' and 'Muddled Minibeasts' by Tony Mitton, and 'Colonel Fazackerley' from *Collected Poems for Children* by Charles Causley, © 1996, Charles Causley (1996, Macmillan).

Graham Denton for the use of 'What a Sucker!' from *Shouting at the Ocean* by Graham Denton. © 2009, Graham Denton (2006, Hands Up Books).

Eddison Pearson for the use of 'Sun a-shine, Rain a-fall'.

Norma Farnes for the use of 'You Must Never Bath in an Irish Stew' and 'A Baby Sardine' by Spike Milligan.

John Foster for the use of 'Uncle Frank' and 'Auntie Arabella'.

Frances Lincoln Ltd for the use of 'Property for Sale' and 'Lice are Nice' from *My Life as a Goldfish* by Rachel Rooney. © 2003, Rachel Rooney (2014, Frances Lincoln).

Gina Maccogy Literary Agency for the use of 'Combinations' from *The Llama Had No Pajama* by Mary Ann Hoberman. © 1976, Mary Ann Hoberman (1998, Houghton Mifflin Harcourt).

David Harmer for the use of 'The Weatherman Forgets His Glasses' from *Big Deal* by David Horner, © 2003, David Horner (2003, BMP Designs), 'Cool at the Pool', 'Trying to Hide the Really Rude SNOG Words', 'Tut-Tut' and 'The Wildebeest'.

International Creative Management for the use of 'Against Broccoli' by Roy Blount, from *Cadbury's 9th Book of Children's Poetry*. © 1991, Roy Blount (1991, Red Fox).

Jean Kenward for the use of 'What's Your Name?'.

Gill McEvoy for the use of 'The Newt'.

Brian Moses for the use of 'Lovesick Snail' and 'Frog Street'.

Joan Poulson for the use of 'Mazey Mary'.

Susan Quinn for the use of 'In Trouble Again'.

John Rice for the use of 'Rhyme-osaur the Dinosaur' and 'Gorbelly Button and his Daddy Gorbelly'.

Rogers, Coleridge and White for the use of 'Three Frazzles in a Frimple' by Brian Patten, from *Juggling with Gerbils* by Brian Patten. © 2000, Brian Patten (2000, Puffin).

Coral Rumble for the use of 'Holiday Print' and 'Baboons' Bottoms'.

Fred Sedgwick for the use of 'What the Headteacher Said When He Saw Me Running Out of School at 1.15 p.m. on 21 July Last Year to Buy an Ice Cream from Pelozzi's Van'.

Andy Seed for the use of 'Spelling Test', 'Unbelievable Sports Facts!' and 'Hindsight'.

Roger Stevens for the use of 'Parent's Evening', 'Advice for Staging Your Own Olympic Games' and 'The Holding Your Breath Contest'.

The Agency (London) for the use of 'Starter' by Tony Bradman.

The Peters Fraser and Dunlop Group for the use of 'George Who Played With A Dangerous Toy' from *Cautionary Tales* by Hilaire Belloc. © 1993, Hilare Belloc (1993, Random House).

Nick Toczek for the use of 'When I Was a Pirate'.

United Agents for the use of 'Hey Diddle Diddle' by Michael Rosen.

Philip Waddell for the use of 'A Tip for Feeding Piranhas' and 'Suddenly – at the Dining Table'.

Celia Warren for the use of 'Moon Theory'.

United Agents for the use of 'Bebe Belinda and Carl Columbus' from *Nothingmas Day* by Adrian Mitchell. © 1984, Adrian Mitchell (1984, Alison & Busby, London).